Alphabets and Images
Inspiration from letterforms

Alphabets and Images
Inspiration from letterforms

Maggie Gordon

Charles Scribner's Sons
New York

Printed in Great Britain
Library of Congress Catalog Card Number 74-7805
ISBN 0-684-14083-7

Contents

Acknowledgment

I would like to thank my husband for his persistent encouragement, my two children for their lively interest in this book, Gerald Woods and Mrs Elliott and their help, Paul Clark for providing material and the following for supplying illustrations of their work:

David Atkinson

Hilary Beck

Peter Bridgewater

Bronwen Careless

Paul Clark

Andrew Cole

Amy-Louise Gordon

Bob Gordon

Patrick Gordon

Mark Jamieson

Charlotte Knox

Valerie Lawrence

Peter Luff

Jacqui McClennan

Michael McNeil

Sue Morley

Paul Munden

Tony Reid

David Rouse

Alan Skinner

Marilyn Tuck

Gerald Woods

Keith Worthington

Chris Wozencraft

Introduction

In compiling this book I have tried to show just a few of the many interesting and varied ways of looking at letterforms. There are of course many, many more, but the intention of producing such a book is to let it act as a springboard for people with ideas of their own. None of the experiments is intended to be commercially functional in any way; they are simply the result of playing with letterforms in particular contexts. For this reason, wherever possible, I have deliberately avoided showing exercises which require the use of sophisticated equipment. Where this is not possible, I have put forward alternative methods.

I hope that the book will be of help and interest to people directly involved with the use of letterforms as shapes, as well as those using them in a more academic sense. It should encourage children to enjoy the letters they have to learn, memorize, read and write at school, as well as to create in most of us an awareness of the interesting letterforms that exist in our immediate surroundings.

Composition using large and small wooden type to make a simple letter pattern with recognizable shapes

Letters as pattern

Counter shape of the letter A

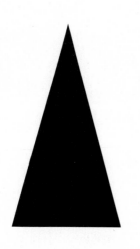

Children when they first become aware of letters see them as abstract shapes and learn that each shape has its own sound. When these are put together they make a collective sound, a word. They can then associate this new shape with something they know or feel through their senses. Shapes arranged collectively produce more words until they grow into whole pages of books.

Forgetting for the moment the letter's sound, concentrate purely on its abstract shape, looking both at the space surrounding the letter and that inside it; in fact explore letterforms from as many different pattern angles as possible.

For most of the exercises shown in this section only simple equipment is needed:
black and white cartridge paper
scissors
scalpel
Cow gum
printing ink
wooden type letters
(If wooden type is not available, the letters required could be cut from strawboard, [*in reverse*], glued onto a base board, inked up and used in the same way as the type.) These ideas can be interpreted in other media as well, using more sophisticated methods.

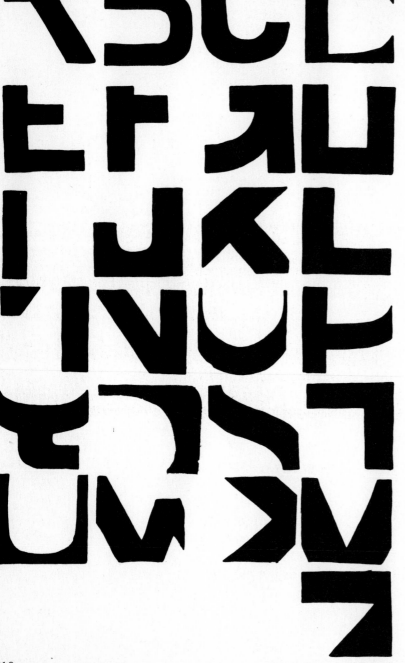

Discovering the critical parts of a letter. The student had to decide which parts to retain in order not to lose the visual identity of each letter of the alphabet

opposite Gradual loss of identity. This was achieved by using only the counter shapes of the letters

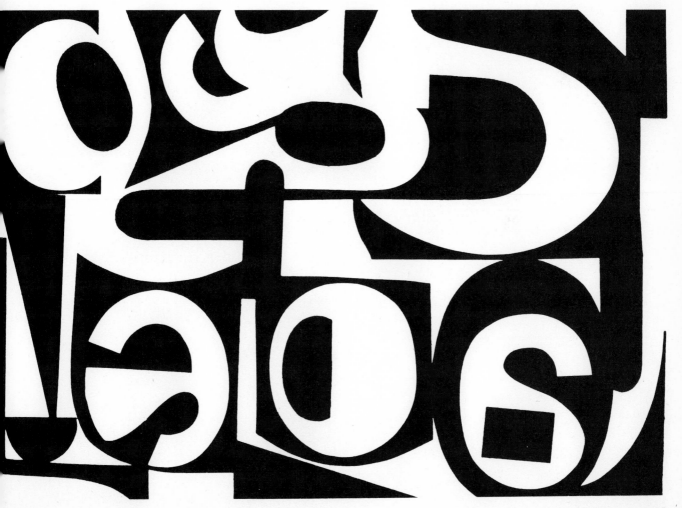

An exercise carried out making use of the
negative form together with contrast in size,
weight, disposition and orientation of the
individual letter forms

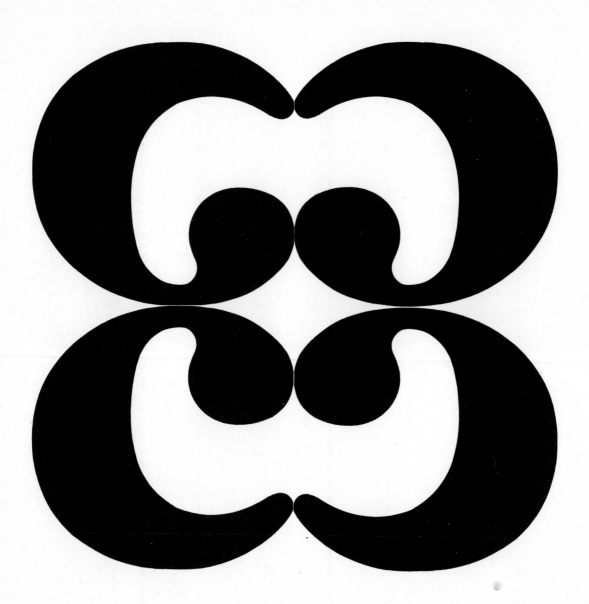

Repetition of the mirrored lower case character c

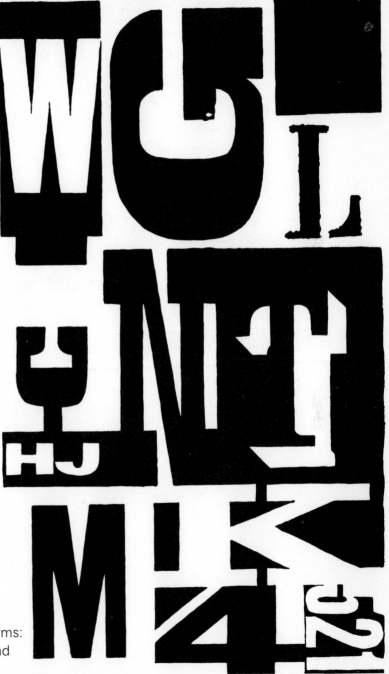

Combined use of different aspects of letterforms:
form, counter form, positive, negative, size and
weight, all used within a defined area

Looking for letterforms

Every day we look at, even if we do not consciously read, the written word. Driving or walking we see sign posts, instructions painted on the road, advertisements or hoardings besides other things that often go unnoticed: a tremendous variety of letterforms in very different contexts. We accept them as part of our life.

The urge to get away from it all may only be a subconscious realization that these products of our urban civilization are so close to us that we feel put upon. The constant bombardment of visual images and information is simply too much.

However, instead of running away from it all this section does just the opposite: it takes a new look at the purely visual side of our immediate surroundings, indeed even to go so far as to make letter shapes from the objects around us, from our own individual environment.

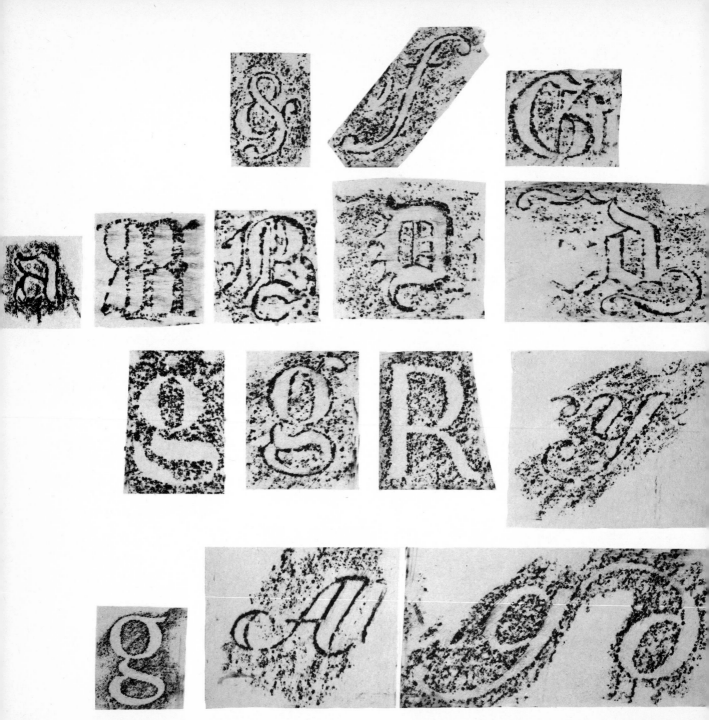

A collection of various rubbings of
letters on buildings and other such
objects

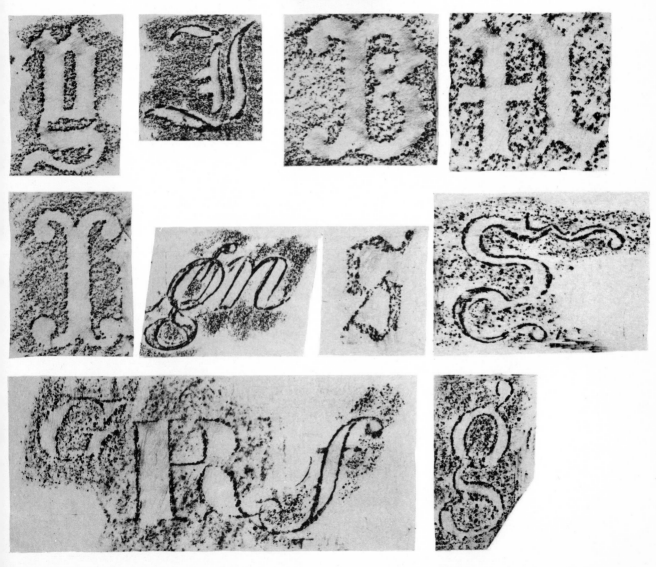

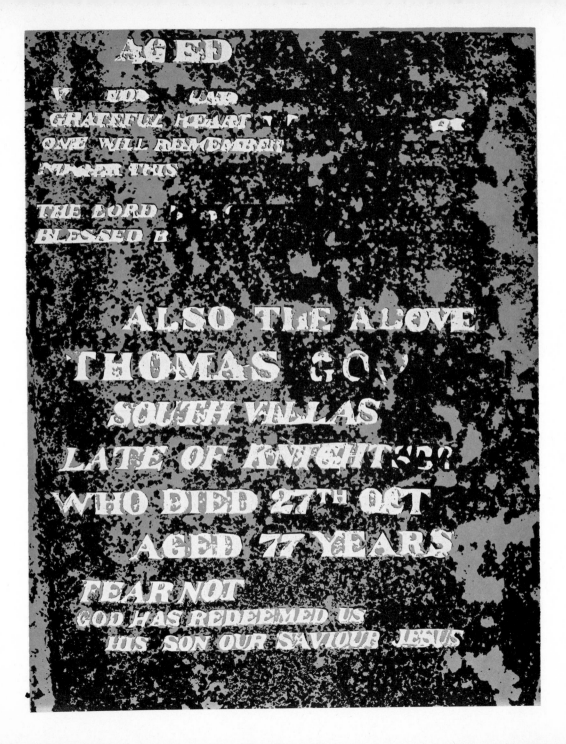

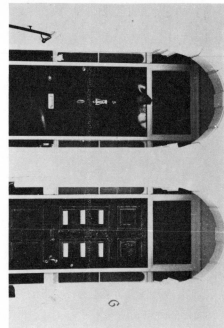

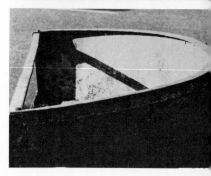

hotographic alphabet
s particular exercise involved, unlike the
vious ones, re-seeing the environment in
h a way that things such as architecture,
fic lights, park benches and walls were
olved into letterforms.

ABCDEFGHIJ
KLMNOPQR
STUVWXYZ
abcdefghijklm
nopqrstuvwxyz

Letters in movement/
Movement within letters

A gradual approach to simple movement with letters arrived at by overprinting and moving the paper vertically

Here are a few of the ways in which movement can be introduced to letterforms both directly and indirectly. Using the characters in pattern form, as opposed to sound symbols, it is possible to create visually various suggestions of movement, eg an action of scattering or throwing, a feeling of speed, the sensation of shifting vertically or horizontally, the feeling of fragmentation or cracking, and the sense of progression or gradual change.

In the following exercises movement is created by using a collection of different or repeated letters, and by a direct movement or change within the letterform itself.

Scattered letters using a spaghetti alphabet

Two examples of slow but
free fragmentation of a
complete alphabet

A composition of printed letters which have been
fragmented in a controlled way using a simple
grid
The composition was first arrived at, a grid then
superimposed. The student subsequently cut
along the grid lines and re-assembled his now
'fragmented' composition using white space to
indicate where the cuts were originally made

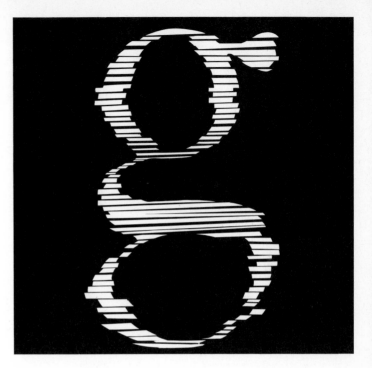

Visual use of horizontal movement within the
letter in order to create a sense of shifting

Slow disintegration of a lower case g

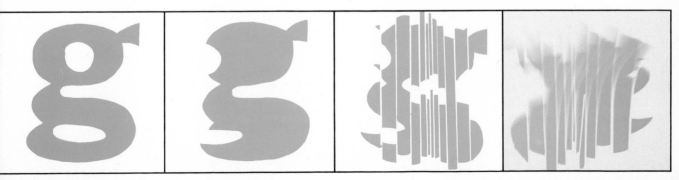

Production of the letter
selected   Disturbance   Disintegration

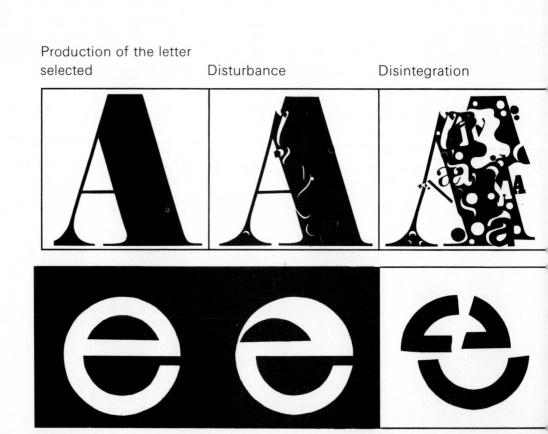

group experimental exercise

iven seven 200 mm squares of paper,
oncertina folded, select a letterform. In square 1
aw the character selected, in square 2 create
sturbance
disintegration
diffusion
re-collection
re-organization
d from this last process, in square 7 evolve a

new symbol. First it is necessary to analyse in
detail subtle differences between the various
processes before attempting to interpret them
visually. One of the exciting things about this
particular experiment is the complete lack of
similarity between any one of the end results,
although they were carried out at the same
time by a group of students, and the marked
visual link between the original character
selected and the new symbol.

iffusion   Re-collection   Re-organization   Evolution of the new symbol

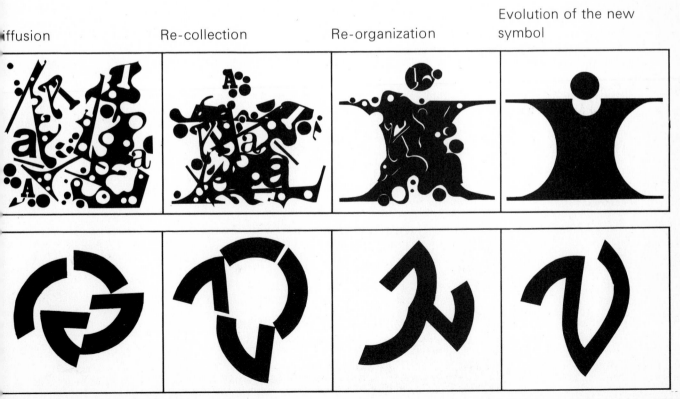

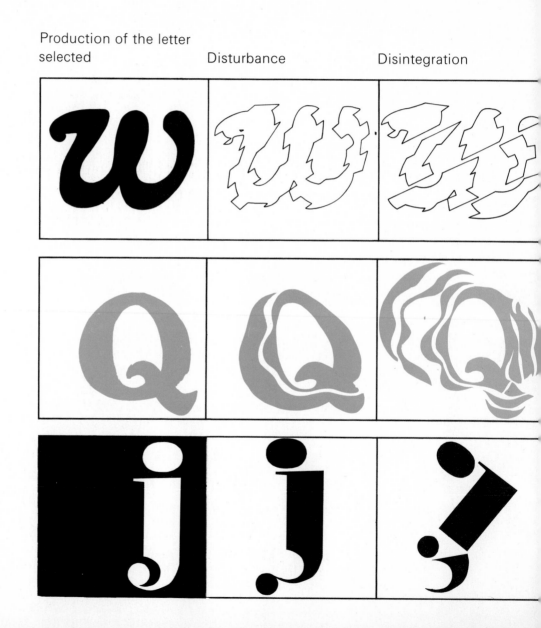

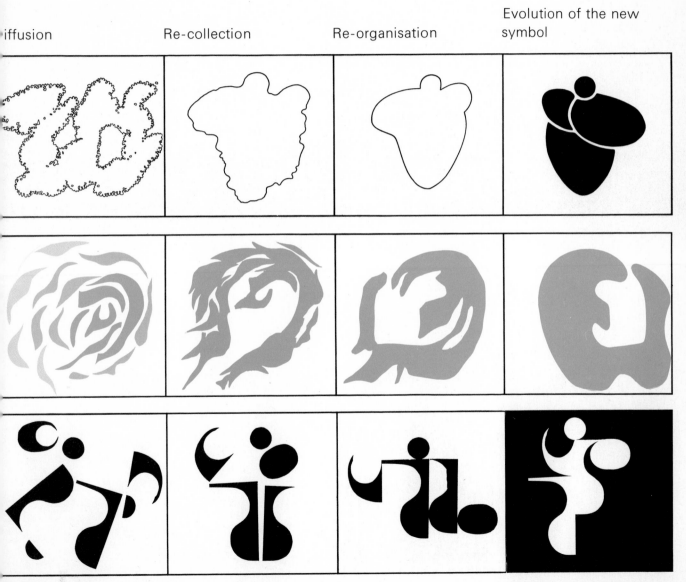

Talking words

Words are a means of communication. When we speak, the listener hears and begins to form his own mental image or sensation of what is being said. When we read, we call upon our imaginatio to visualize the content matter. Naturally no two readers form exactly the same image.

In this section certain words have been treated in such a way that they have taken on the visual appearance of their meaning. This 'appearance' can be achieved in various ways: by using size, shape, pattern, texture, disposition, space, various methods of printing, colour, doodling, hand lettering and many other techniques. However, before treating words in this way, a thorough understanding of the actual word is needed. So often we think we understand the meaning of a commonplace word, and it is not until such an experiment is undertaken that we fully realize that a much deeper comprehension of the word is needed before we can hope to communicate to others what we ourselves so clearly have in mind.

45

spidery

Hi

DREAM

TWELVE O CLOCK

a whole heap of YELLING YELLING YELLING YELLING YELLING YELLING YELLING YELLING YELLING

46

GLASS

NEWS

CH.e.M.C.i.C.a.L

BRANDY SNAPS

eclair

Old new

alive ൧൦൧൦

WIDE narrow

BIG SMALL

QUIET loud

SOLID crack

crowd alone

51

Talking text

When listening to favourite songs, opera or conversations with a particular accent or dialect, it is interesting to visualize in what sort of pattern we would write down the words or how the tonal qualities could be interpreted.

It is easier to carry out such an exercise with a song or accent that has a great personal fascination, one that you feel you understand intimately. When awareness and understanding of free typographic interpretation has developed, it is a challenge to try this with a given text. The two following pages show examples of free personal typographic renderings of typical English and American 'communications'. With the two subsequent illustrations of song interpretation, it is exciting to listen to the music and follow the words of the song as they have been interpreted here.

"Well you know, *it's sort of,* I mean, *well* you know, it's SORT OF, YOU KNOW, I MEAN, well sort of, *you know, it's well sort of.....* [*I agree!*]

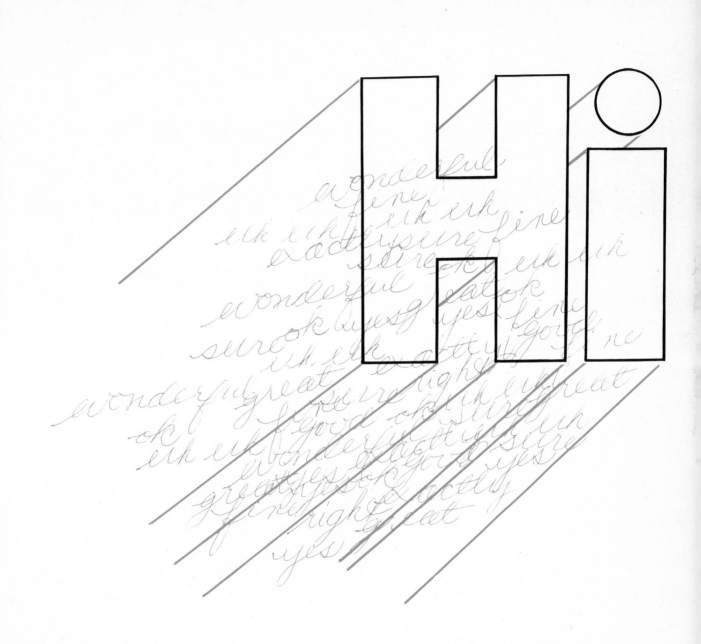

Old Ebenezer thought he was JULIUS CAESAR

and so they put him in a h o me

where they gave him

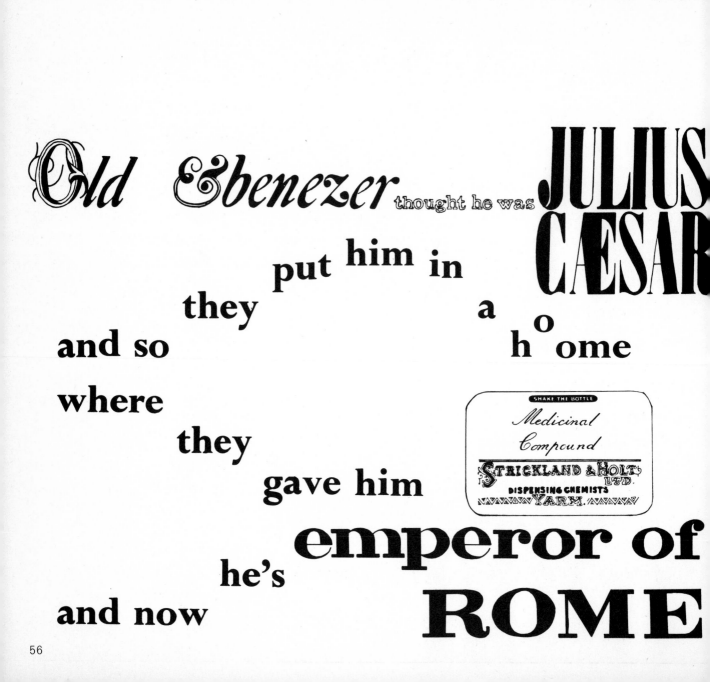

SHAKE THE BOTTLE

Medicinal Compound

STRICKLAND & HOLT LTD.

DISPENSING CHEMISTS YARM.

and now he's emperor of ROME

HEY JUDE don't make it BAD

take a Sad song —

and make it BET———TER

REMEMBER TO LET HER IN-TO YOUR HEART

THEN YOU CAN START

to make it———————BETTER———

AND ANY-TIME YOU FEEL THE PAIN

HEY JUDE refrain

don't CAR———RY THE WORLD

UPON YOUR SHOUL-DERS

FOR WELL YOU KNOW THAT IT'S A FOOOL

Who plays it COOL

By mak - ing his WORLD

a lit-tle cold-er ___

da da da da da da da

57

is not for apple

Emotive letters

is for apple

We are so used to taking for granted the sound symbol aspect of letterforms that the emotive content is often missed.

The illustration on the facing page is typical of many seen in children's educational books. We readily accept that this is an A just like any other A, only in this particular case it is identified with 'Apple'. The shape of this A has little visual regard for the object chosen: an apple, which is round in shape, physically tangible, crisp and refreshing in taste. Were this A representing the word 'Angle' it would convey the geometric qualities extremely well visually. The lower case conveys a great deal more 'apple feel'.

There are many ways of exploring this particular aspect of the letterform. To start with the subject matter should be kept simple in order to have a more direct visual appeal in the end result. However, as we become more aware and sensitive to letterforms, and are prepared to spend time researching into the feel and meaning of the subject matter, a complete personal alphabet, along the lines of that shown on pages 64 to 71 could be devised.

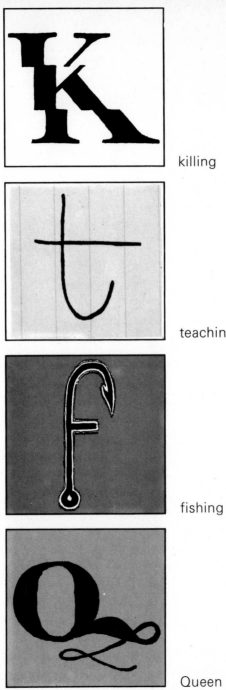

killing

teaching

fishing

for night

Queen

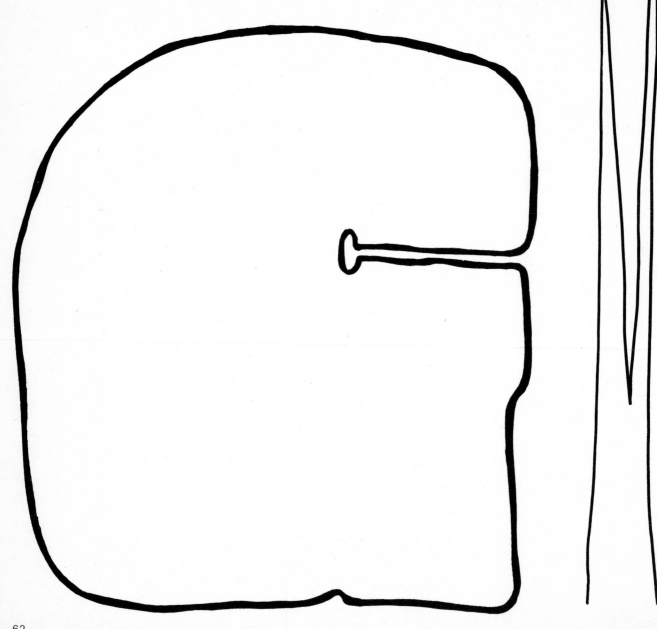

An adults' alphabet

ambiguity

boredom

B B B B B B B
B B B B
B B B
B B
B
B
B

contentment

depreciation

D

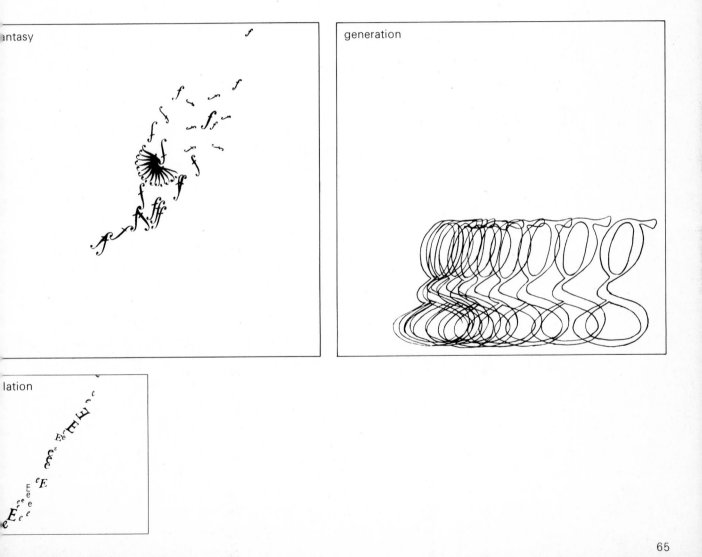

fantasy

generation

lation

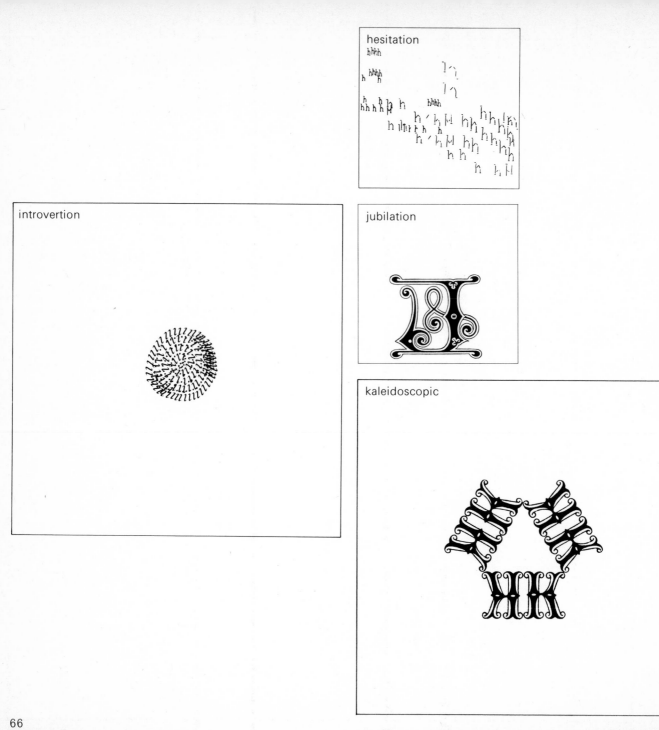

hesitation

introvertion

jubilation

kaleidoscopic

memory

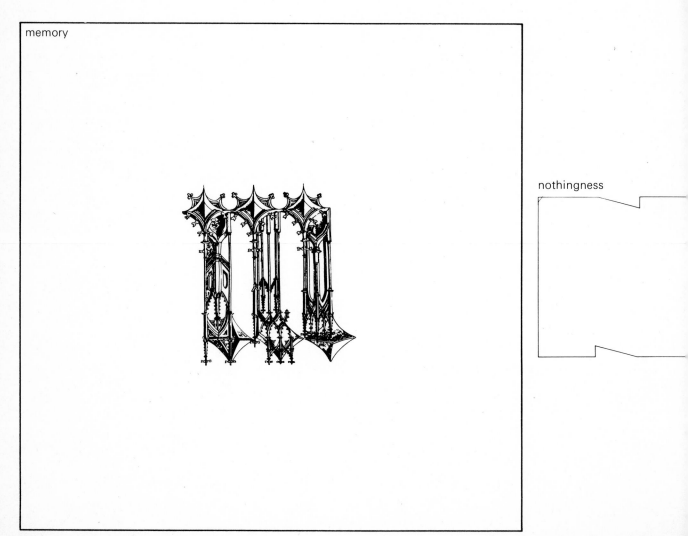

nothingness

oblivion

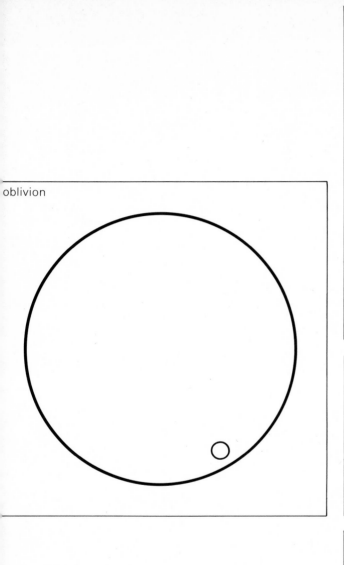

purification

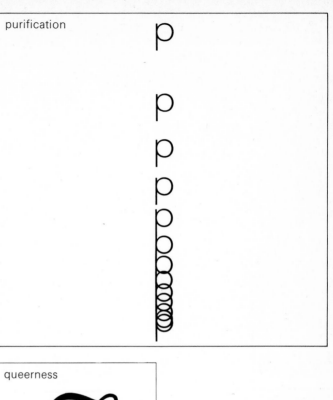

queerness

retrospection

schizophrenic

unconsciousness

terrorization

verbosity

wantonness

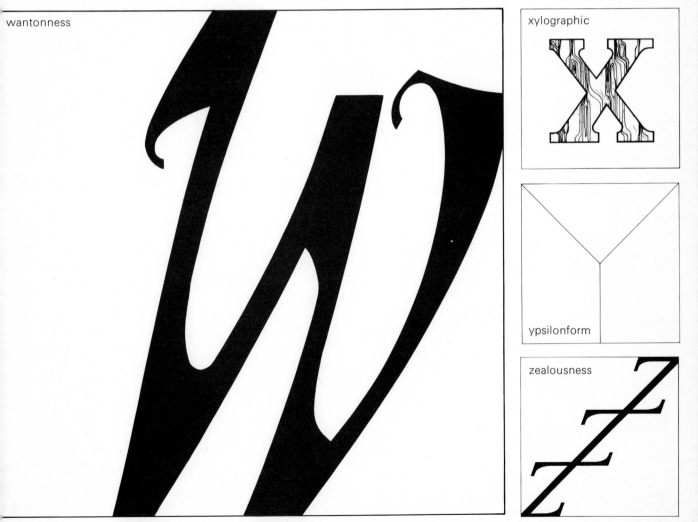

xylographic

ypsilonform

zealousness

```
       "Fury said to
         a mouse, That
            he met in the
               house, 'Let
                  us both go
                     to law: I
                        will prose-
                           cute you.
                        Come, I'll
                     take no de-
                  nial; We
               must have
            a trial:
         For really
      this morn-
   ing I've
nothing
to do.'
   Said the
      mouse to
         the cur,
            'Such a
               trial, dear
                  Sir, With
                     no jury
                        or judge,
                           would
                           be wast-
                        ing our
                     breath.'
                  'I'll be
               judge,
            I'll be
         jury,'
      Said
   cun-
   ning
   old
      Fury:
         'I'll
            try
            the
               whole
                  cause,
                     a n d
                        con-
                        demn
                     you to
                  death.'"
```

Mass and texture

In this context, *mass* is defined as a collection of printed matter: in newspapers, magazines and books, as well as any collection of writing: exercise books, letters and shopping lists; and *texture* as the visual feel of the surface presented by this mass. Being concerned with the actual content of 'mass', we tend to miss the visual textural quality. In this section the emphasis is placed on the exciting visual effect. Exploration into mass can be taken a stage further by relating the total content to the finished visual effect as so clearly indicated by the example on the left.

Simple handwriting when used as the only material for a collage gives a lively, uneven visual texture.

man out of peices. I
and is just what he
pain in aswell. One night
some lightning struck
the Frankenstien
tion when it stopped
to the ground. professer
over wanted to make a
her side of the world
name was professer
make two twins I said
"cula" so he did. But

my cousonn
Having a good.
apart from a
wind screen, van
+ mosquito

Viking edge - men
1000 and AD 105
sille Fjord were
of barriers to
the five Viking
town of Roo
are

Shepherd,
can't come now I
If you don't come now they wil
Shepherd
Shephe
Drer
So Daddy isn't here
you will be doing.
his job inste Frankenstien
I wonder Sne I will make
will be Frankenstien put a
I did eny ard Just then
he came
professer Franken

On top of it
Nikolayevich Rusanov had never been and could
but his heart sank when the
and. They should ha
chirtren to some th

upon tim the
woman and
man and
livd in a
new nay

Once I built a
a great tall on
I built it out of
I dressed him in
And I called hi

When we look at unfamiliar alphabets, our eyes are forced to view initially the purely textural quality.

A more exacting exercise is to divide a given area into equal squares and fill these with varied textures of printed matter in order to create a sense of planes lying flat, projecting and receding

Russian

Идя навстречу требованиям жизни и по желаниям наших читателей, мы изменяемся, расширяемся и совершенствуемся.

Стремясь решить труднейшую задачу удовлетворения запросов самых разнообразных категорий читателей, мы освещаем широкий круг вопросов: печатное дело, оформление, история, археология философия, поэзия и даже незатейливые приключенческие рассказы из жизни джунглей. Когда мы оглядываемся назад то мы ищем вдохновения для будущего. Когда мы глядим вперед, то мы надеемся помочь кампании за модернизацию печат

Arabic

لقد توسعنا وتغيرنا ونأمل أن نكون تحسنا. فى عام
تغير الأذواق واجهنا مشكلة لم تكن معروفه لسلفنا
هى محاولة إرضاء إن لم يكن إدخـال السرور على
طبقات كثيرة من القراء فى شتى الموضوعات :
فلسـفـة وتاريخ ، فكاهة وغموض ، شعر ، تصميم
وطباعة. و۵ نهمل تطبيق العلم والمسرح فى عصرنا هذا.
ولقـد استوحينا من ما ضيناحـاضرنا. وعند ما
ننظر الى هـذا المستقبل نؤمن بهذا التصنيع القادم
والمساهون معنـا رغم إختلافهم سيكونـون صورة
مصغرة لعالم عديد الجنسيات مثل هذنا.
أننا نود أن نتحدث مع قرائنا كل بلغته ومقال
يقدم بأكبر عدد من اللغات على قدر ما يسمح به
المكان و إنا لنعتذر عما يترك رغم إرادتنا.

Hindi

Greek

Ἐτροποποιήσαμεν, ἐπεξετείναμεν καί ἐ
τιώσαμεν τάς ἐκδόσεις μας ὥστε νά ἀ
ποκρίνονται πρός τάς ἀξιώσεις τῆς ἐπ
μας καί τάς προσδοκίας τῶν ἀναγνωστῶν
Πρός Ἱκανοποίησιν τῆς μεγάλης ποικιλίας
ἀναγνωστῶν μας, περιελάβομεν εἰς τάς ἐπ
σεις μας μίαν εὐρεῖαν ποικιλίαν θεμά
τυπογραφίαν, σχεδίασμα, Ἱστορίαν, ἀρχ
λογίαν, φιλοσοφίαν, ποίησιν, ἀκόμη δέ
ἀστυνομικά μυθιστορήματα δαιδαλώδ
πλοκῆς. Στρέφοντες τά βλέμματά μας εἰς
παρελθόν ἀναζητοῦμεν ἐμπνεύσεις διά τό
λον. Προσβλέποντες δέ εἰς τό μέλλον ἐλπίζο
ὅτι συμβάλλομεν εἰς τό γενικόν αἴτημα διά

74

house and g...arrel is where the ...ht whiskies slumber...ish air reaching th... maturity. At just the... these are brought... Cutty Sark. Then, in...us liquid straight...

ic throughout...uber recitals a...in the house...erts are given...

at 10/- (50p) pe... plus postage and... packing at Xp In... London postal a... Xp elsewhere. *enclose cash/c... postal order to the...*

Bishop of Worcester... later to be accused... the health of the P... sat to Reynolds... st May, 1773. There... r 1774, but a second... was made for the...

TO SEE *Chelsea Ph...* *...den is open to ...* ...5, 5–8 this Friday a... *with stamped addre...* ...day and period yo... the Committee, Mr E... ...et Street, London E...

team will support o... ng promotions and exc... also to the Chemist, Gr... also envisaged that... the vacant established... they arise. As suc...

Jan – Fiat 850. Fe... & Midget. Mar... A40. Jul – Triumph... ...mbridge. Oct – Su... n DS TD. Dec – For... — MGB. July – Su... Sep – Volkswagen... Nov – Volvo 131 &... ar – Jaguar Mk 1...

Lancaster ...ll-colour c... /14 section... ...d Survey

The unique gu... great reputation... tells you what... know about the... and detailed re... 250 recommend... cluding some... and much expe...

bread rolls, caref... over the screw... handouts and th... cables on the the hotel ma... a whispered of... briefing to... pondents in the two waitresses...

...eeds of London... O roads and st... day 10,000 jou... ding 1,000 on e... the new amb... s into operatio... nable control.

most attention i... ere those matters... orations doing bus... the European eco... nds. Interest rate... ge rules and restri... ere is no doubt wha... speaking the 10% ra... se the cost of runni... charge which in s... hour will be increas... ns servicing and repa... expensive and, of c... accessories and ... es will likewise incre...

the other end... ple who want... ituation. They... t. They want... just in case. In... every feature ...

(TOPS), which w... opportunities for... employment, this... The Associati... involvement of t... about the project... inadequate. True

stored and o... of an English... and painting... during the project... clude Cleopa...

ENGR: J Watson... COLL: Mrs Emp... 27th May, 1909 (... 1909, by whom pr... LIT: Chaloner Sr... *Portraits,* 1884, Vo... Williamson, *John ...* attrib. to Zoffany...

true this pen wo... marital status. B... man with the se... his own way, a... ng. And the fac... ord puzzles in th... courage far be... then he's using...

Art Colleges ...to be operated... ussed by the ...ere been any... aing Bodies or... dway College... t in September

3 × 86 mm. 2791 cc. OHC... ...2·07 × 106 mm. 4235 cc. OH... ...ced. Available with choice o... engines and either manual o... fully automatic transmission... round. High performance... ervo-assisted disc brakes on... Alternator. Full luxur... assisted steering and... ventilation system with... lective automatic temp. co... positive air extraction.

...uthority for G... ic policies in th... ework of the... and Local G... cils and the C... ns. Co-operati

...ACKED plates, col... bliging staff and h... es seem to be a fe... most restaurants... don. Yet I seem to com... customer to comp... the British public is... otten what it is lik... good, well-cooked... lean surroundings.

...by Osber... nd superb f... own house... Listing a

of *Paintings in the Palace* II, p127. *National Portrait Exhib...* tish Museum, *Wilkes...* sibly the 'fine picture... bited in 1768, and at... 1771 (125). *Ministry of Public Buil...*

up an appetite in th... Play some tennis or h... delicious dinner at t... rooftop restaurant o... tic San Juan. Try you... tables of our governm... casino. Dance all nig... studded revue of int... advancement with thi... ing Company are exce... of our Senior Industri... personnel man will b... at the address show... 2.00 p.m. and 8.00 p... the Reception Desk f...

Behn was born in... nds when they... l by Denmark;... Danish and his mo... and he was bro... polyglot backgro... Sosthenes, with... nand, quickly lo... and the readings co... iest known portrait... painted in 1732, a... Pope's favourite... ' at the age of 28. to John Holliday,... Inn, Fellow of the... author of the first I... for which it was

uses of language and... learning. The contribu... and sociologists are p... represent their respec... controversies about l... the educationally dis... tions of the psycholog... s debate emerge w...

ughts get put t... s why Ellswor... anking Depart... Along with J... trader. And Jo... desk. Alfred H... : cricket is a ser... West Indies, co... ...pad in the Barba... l the pavilion is... batting side wa... ile the other field... frequently inter...

lawyers, the ...ho commission... magnificent city... s divided into are... ...functional group... ...re,' he expalined... ...uying it and t... keepers there, de...

213 Park Ave. S.,... The upstairs portion... r palace is furnished... temporary, and the pl... rrespondingly contem... ve, a far-out electronic... is in its musicality... ear through Sunday... Tuesdays are devoted... s and rocksters, after... (to two) people may i...

Arrangements for the... administrative staff o... Authority, including r... pay, conditions of ser... promotion schemes... accommodation, pub... relations, museums... education library.

elegant, functional tap... best we've seen. Ma... ed stainless, steel, he... ng loaded 10 ft. rule... and inches but also... Hairline reading win... d-out. It's also a squar... bubble gauge. Retrac... es or draw circles. Gua... ve ever owned or Yo... der by mail or visit the

and commer... the depart... of Housing a... official bodi... mbie Award... nternational L...

vis has an ea... ..., you call f... orm will be... imply show... way in your

police force — to 's... numbers and r... ment' — would be... tenacity and resol... s way we are fo... ment that Franc... ncluded: 'In a larg...

Primary and secondar... education including... teaching staff in schoo... (except interviews for... teachers), non-teachi... staff, employment of... children, safety, health... welfare of pupils, fina...

There never was more... opinion of the judges were... All the seats were never... never happened before, d... the 11th day of Novembe... never has appeared in co... opinion: every rule, orde... have been unanimous.'

ndard (Fury, Polara, ... ermediate (Satellite... nomy (Duster, Dem... you normally purcha... as part of your renta... you normally purchas... your rentals? □Yes

ICE IS HEREBY GIVE... the 8th June 1973 David... n duly authorised in tha... Clarence Commissions (B... ited whose registered o... Ganton House, Ganton... don, W1A 2LD, and for... lf of the said Company... Lnbrokes The Bookma... application to the... sing Committee for th... r Upon Thames Petty S... sion for the grant of a... Licence in respect of p... 37, Lower Richmond... S.W.14.

keeps before it that... ts who wish to... and push-chair... hibitions, but h... ly to the decision... being blocked in p... so great where... congregate that...

able as a Granad... rip and the du... to the body pan... r. Made both in... onsul/Granada... /Zodiac series,... ny. The cars are... powered by di...

ntian circumstar... capes were influ... by *Hadleigh C*... ressionists. It is... onstable's own in...

olitics. His bank acc... rticular ball pen do... rprising number of... Its clean lines tell y... nctional design. An... now the sterling silv... tense. He knows if

"All right—but s... sed it only to esca... ate husband who... im in the bedroom... ife. The gimmick... evalued by the use... — not Bondian, old... It is this feeling... light and honourabl... Kept Bond films

scape style owes... ...ut the colour is h... ...ires are marked o... of simplicity of s... of the Persian s...

you wear wit... is not too im... platform shoes,... sneakers, beard... s are acceptable. y, Billy Murphy... s-hand 1950's f... at he sells for a... g on the garis...

ation is gettin... y, the police a... use violence... violence. They e... violence. In... ...e are presen...

dicates those pr... ossible for wheel-... on occasions. I... ent accept them... ust at all times

respect, and a rep... politics. His bank...

LL: Presented to Chri... reton prior to 1798. : J Gutch, *Appendix* t... *tory and Antiquities of th... ford,* 1790, p290; Histo... III, pp89–90, rep: M...

r: Vandergucht; Vert... ...ept Bond films

75

As well as using the organised nature of the typewriter to make rigidly controlled letterforms, by freeing the 'paper grip' unexpected results occur.

safeguard the existing flood defences along the ba
hours or perhaps as late as four hours before high
trigger the start of a countdown for barrier closur
misery and suffering. The moral is obvious — it jus
also minimises interference with amenity. The diag
been done to give more protection where the risk i
height. In fact some emergency wall raising has al
the warning would either be cancelled or confirme
greatest. Most of these temporary defences could
cost and speed of construction over the other typ
without taking into account the cost of life, sheei

If very abnormal weather conditions coincide witl
used to bring the barrier into action. This provide:
could paralyse the central part of the undergroun
to the problem it offers tremendous advantages in
government buildings. No one can assess the prol
and could knock out power, gas and water suppli
thousands of homes, shops, factories, businesses
telephone and teleprinter services and severely hi
tide there would be a flood disaster in London wh
give the usual advance warning to shipping. Poss
the operating machinery until in the fully raised p
the sector gates are swung up out of their housin
sight in their housings on the river bed. In an eme
average high tides at London Bridge are currently
requirements — and when not in use the gates are
show the construction of the barrier. The four ma
Because the Thames could turn into a killer overn
general tides are rising. The combined effect is su
design is already going ahead and will take about

TYPOGRAPHIC

Looking at actual lines of type, we can
see where white space has been allowed to play
a part in the completed experiment. This has
been achieved in both random and controlled
ways.

TYPOGRAPHICTYPOGRAPHICTYPOGRAPHICTYPOGRAPHIC

TYPOGRAPHICTYPOGRAPHICTYPOGRAPHICTYPOGRAPHIC

ness of fit. In a serifed – especially a slab-serife
eness of fit can present problems: there is a tend
nserifed, rounded characters to appear loose. In
ockwell, this fault has been largely avoided.
cent serifs all but touch, such characters as b, c, d,
q do not spoil the even flow of the line. This is due
extra width and height of the rounded parts of thes
h allow them amply to fill their respective position
ying attention to the inter-character space. It is po
ise individual combinations of letters – no type de
erfect on this score – but the overall appearance
rs, and in this respect Rockwell is particularly suc
hat purpose then can Rockwell serve us today?
of the excessive use of sanserifs in jobbing work
ed face of the style of Rockwell can offer a pleasing
It may be less readable – always a difficult point to
rove – and one cannot visualise its being suitable
gs, but it remains a clear, closely-fitting, well-in
Its family is nicely balanced, and its monoline ch
lend themselves to photomechanical reproducti

il the even flow of the line
nd height of the rounded
amply to fill their respe
to the inter-character
al combinations of letter
is score – but the overa
his respect Rockwell is p
then can Rockwell serv
ssive use of sanserifs in
e style of Rockwell can o

er-character
tions of letter
but the over
Rockwell is p
Rockwell ser

ns of l
the c
ckwel

Radically enlarging a defined area of type allows the reader to become aware of the size and texture of the mass content.

Strange atmospheres can be evoked by particula
placing of printed matter, using colour and
movement.

At the end of the war London faced an acute housing
shortage. No new building had taken place for six
years and many people had lost
bombing: couples married younger during the
wartime and wanted to set up home on their own.
The LCC had put
(prefabs) on vac
but it was always intended that these would
y a temporary palliative for the crisis. Un-
fortunately, these temporary homes used up many up emergency factory made houses
of the vacant sites
Council began to look beyond the city's boundaries
for space to build its per
held what were for a County
to build houses both inside an,
boundaries but it also faced a rehousing problem ant sites and on the edges of

that was unique in its size—hundreds of thousands their homes
of people needed new homes. Over the next few
years a number of large low-density
estates' were built outside the
while the redevelopment progr
London was getting under way, until, by 1960 in the
nearly 100,000 people had mo
war houses. Harold Hill and Aveley are but tw
examples. During this time the Gover
introducing legislation to help cope with the crisis.

Under the New Towns Act, 1946 eight new towns,
each with an estimated population of 25,000 or more within the London area a
were designated to meet the needs of Greater London. nd the
In 1952 this
ment Act to encourage and
of existing towns by agreement between local parks,
authorities. By 1962 the LCC had signed sixteen outside
town expansion agreeme
thirty and sixty miles from London. Eventually amme in inner
these sixteen enlarged towns would house 50,000 nts for towns bet
ex-London families. However, realising that these
old established towns

thrust upon them and that the pace of develop
would be relatively slow, the LCC in the mid-
fifties asked the Government for permission to ment
prepare a scheme in parallel
a new town of 100,000 people with

and Local Government began to urge the release of
government and railway surplus lands as part of the ween
drive to solve the London housing problem. This with these solutions for
initiative identified and mapped out a ring of practi-manent houses.
cally empty sites, which could be released to re- was reinforced by the T
house people, area by area,
boroughs so that works of redevelopment could from the crowded inner
... The sites included Hendon and Council unique power

jazz rhythm swing melody tempo beat tune blues pop mood rave
jazz rhythm swing melody tempo beat tune blues pop mood rave
jazz rhythm swing melody tempo beat tune blues pop mood rave
jazz rhythm swing melody tempo beat tune blues pop mood rave
jazz rhythm swing melody tempo beat tune blues pop mood rave
jazz rhythm swing melody tempo beat tune blues pop mood rave
jazz rhythm swing melody tempo beat tune blues pop mood rave
jazz rhythm swing melody tempo beat tune blues pop mood rave
jazz rhythm swing melody tempo beat tune blues pop mood rave
jazz rhythm swing melody tempo beat tune blues pop mood rave
jazz rhythm swing melody tempo beat tune blues pop mood rave
jazz rhythm swing melody tempo beat tune blues pop mood rave
jazz rhythm swing melody tempo beat tune blues pop mood rave
jazz rhythm swing melody tempo beat tune blues pop mood rave
jazz rhythm swing melody tempo beat tune blues pop mood rave
jazz rhythm swing melody tempo beat tune blues pop mood rave
jazz rhythm swing melody tempo beat tune blues pop mood rave
jazz rhythm swing melody tempo beat tune blues pop mood rave
jazz rhythm swing melody tempo beat tune blues pop mood rave
jazz rhythm swing melody tempo beat tune blues pop mood rave
jazz rhythm swing melody tempo
jazz rhythm swing melody

Atmospheric conditions such as sun radiation, fog and rain can be emulated by using various printed or typed letters.

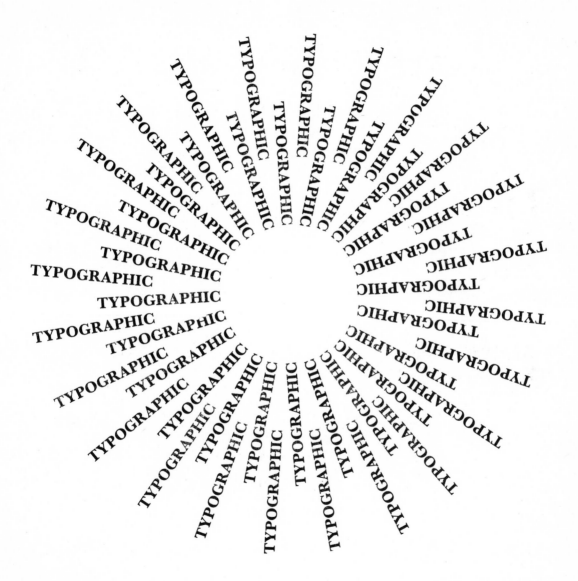

A man-hole cover is interpreted here in hand drawn 'i's

An abstract pattern made from cash register bills giving an interesting tonal quality

A symbolic forest created by using a rubber date
stamp

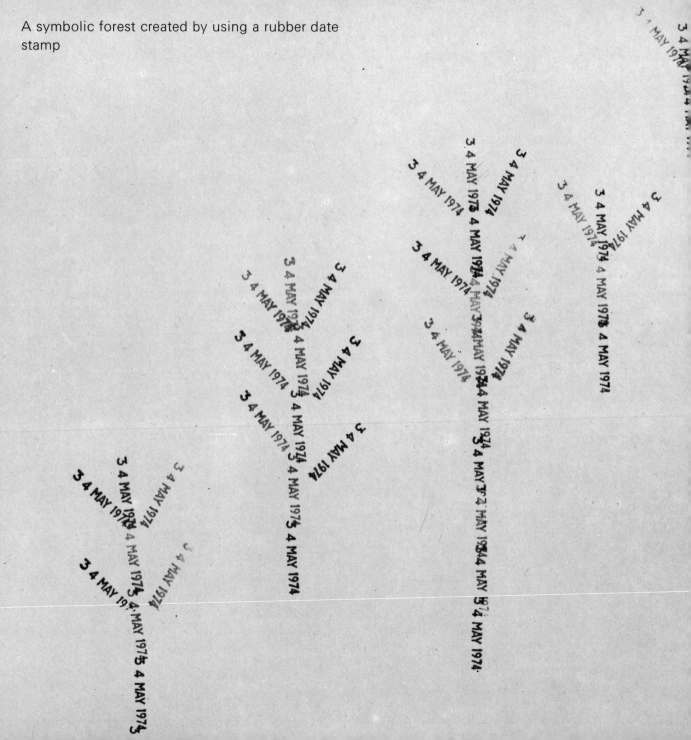

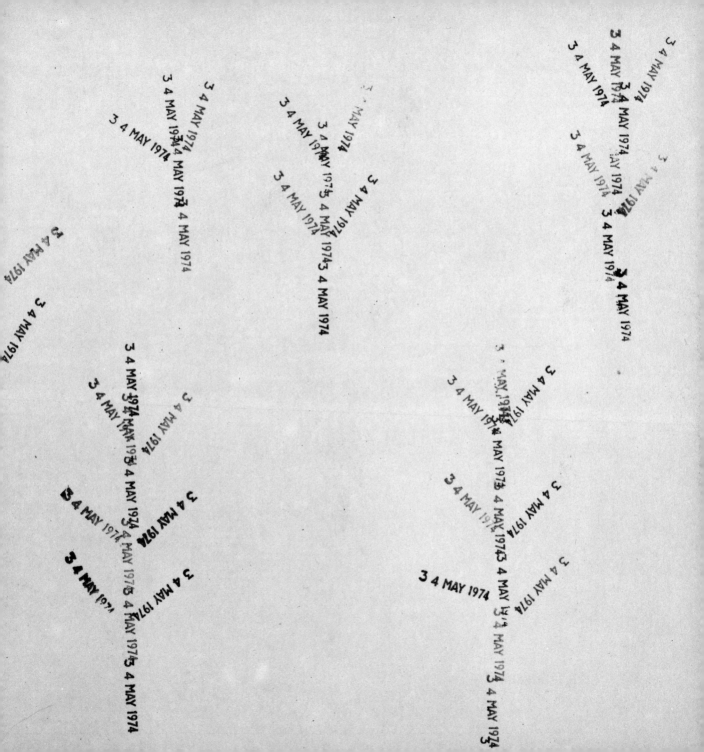

A typographic rendering of a piece of hand-wov
herring-bone tweed has the same visual 'feel'
as the cloth itself

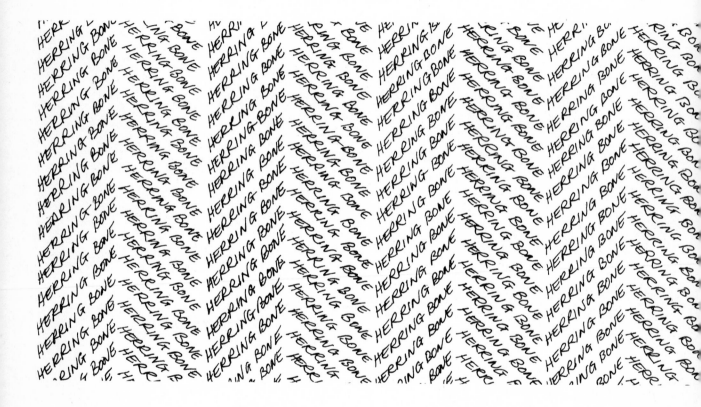

The quality of wrought iron work is evoked
through the abstract arrangement of suitable
letterforms

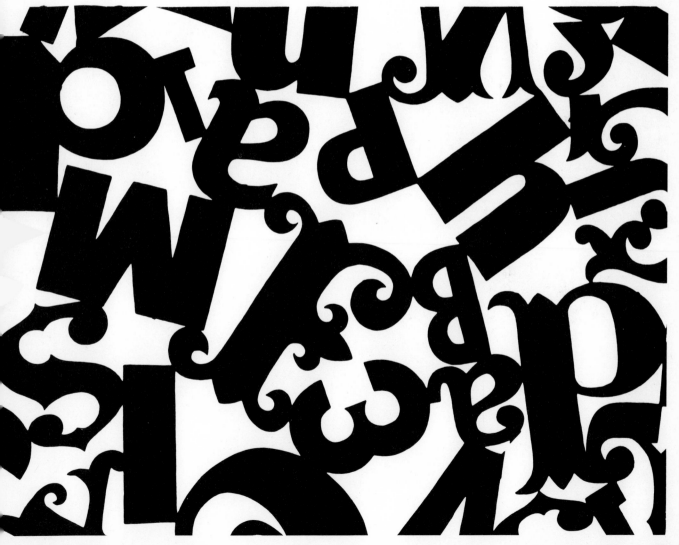

A typographic sea created by using wooden type, hand inking it, and printing it manually in the most evocative position

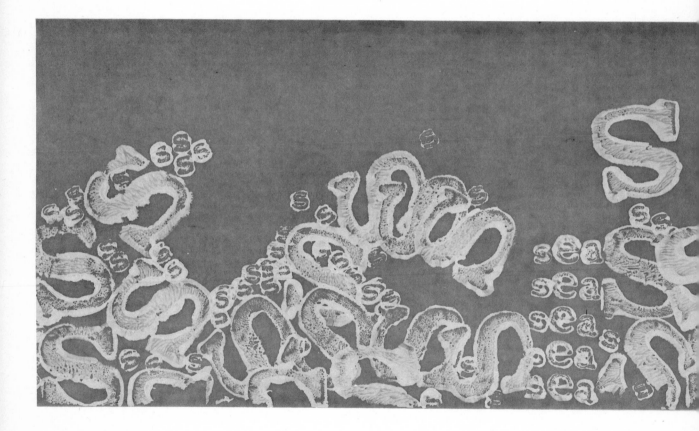

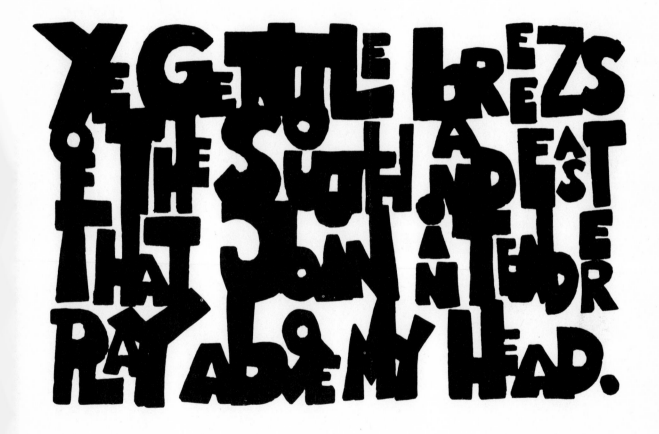

Bright clean blue sky

Pure white smokey trailing clouds

dusting

Ragged grassy hill
covered in dusty purple
cross-stitch patches

thin acid slither of sharp green

musky
petrified
trees

dusty green
mound

Materials

Basic equipment
Scissors
Craft knife or razor blades
Straight edge
Pair of compasses
Set square
Mapping pen
Lettering pen
Pen nibs including italic ones
Instant lettering
Black and white cartridge papers
Tracing paper
Adhesives
Washable lettering ink
Indian ink
Coloured inks
White ink
Assorted colours of gouache or poster paints, including black and white
Selection of sable hair brushes

Additional useful materials
Instant lettering catalogues
Lino for lino cuts and cutting tools
Potatoes for potato cuts
Any rubber stamps
Inking pad
Ink roller *gelatine*
Tissue paper *a range of colours*
Gummed paper *a range of colours*
Coloured cartridge papers
Stencil kit
Coloured fibre-tip pens
Dictionary
Type specimen book
Camera
Note book
Scrap book for visual notes
Wax crayons for rubbings
Graph paper
Blotting paper
Coloured film for overlaying
Typewriter

Possible sources of finding material
Newspapers
Magazines
Comic books
Labels
Posters
Exercise books
Tickets
Programmes

Adhesives
Cow Gum (rubber cement)   Good for all lightweight papers
Easy to remove with lighter fuel
Spray adhesive   Very good for sticking large areas of tissue paper
PVA   Sticks things edge to edge very well
Copydex   Suitable for most things especially fabrics and collage. Can be removed with amyl acetate
Polycell (wallpaper paste)   Useful for collage work as it dries clear
Balsa cement   Good for 3D work.
NB   Impact adhesives are not suitable for paper work.

Suppliers

Most of the items mentioned are available at any good art store and large stationers or from the following specialists:

Artists materials and equipment

E J Arnold Limited
School Suppliers
Butterley Street
Leeds LS10 1AX

Reeves and Sons Limited
Lincoln Road
Enfield, Middlesex

Winsor and Newton Limited
Wealdstone
Harrow, Middlesex

Papers

G F Kettle
127 High Holborn
London W1

Paperchase Limited
216 Tottenham Court Road
London W1

Instant lettering

Letraset Shop
44 Gerard Street
London W1
A comprehensive catalogue available

DATE

APR 14

JAN 8